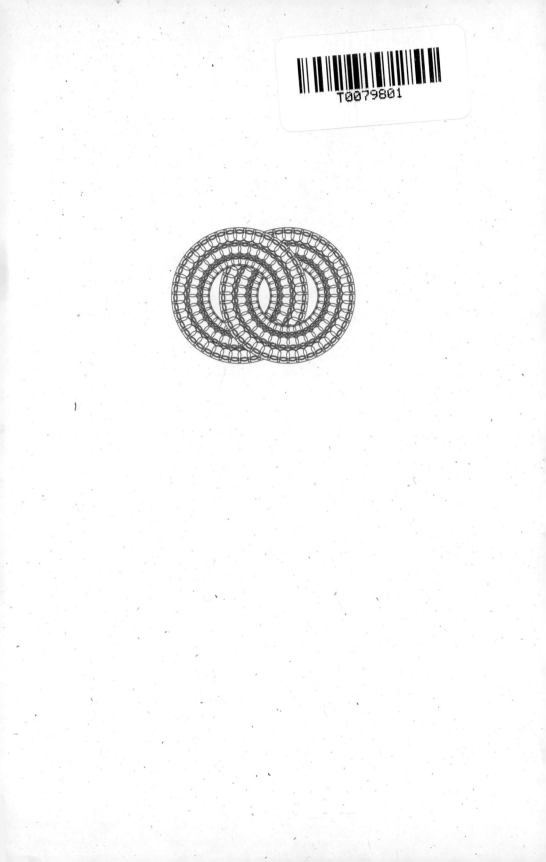

Wonderama

WON DER AMA

Catherine Doty

CAVANKERRY
PRESS

CavanKerry Press Ltd.
Fort Lee, New Jersey
www.cavankerrypress.org

Publisher's Cataloging-In-Publication Data
(Prepared by The Donohue Group, Inc.)
Names: Doty, Catherine, author.
Title: Wonderama / Catherine Doty.
Other Titles: Won der ama
Description: First edition. | Fort Lee, New Jersey : CavanKerry Press, 2021.
Identifiers: ISBN 9781933880822
Subjects: LCSH: Poor children—New Jersey—Paterson—Poetry. | Coming of age—
    Poetry. | Nineteen sixties—Poetry. | American poetry—21st century. | LCGFT:
    Poetry.
Classification: LCC PS3604.O88 W66 2020 | DDC 811/.6—dc23

Cover photograph provided by the author
Cover and interior text design by Ryan Scheife, Mayfly Design
First Edition 2021, Printed in the United States of America

CavanKerry Press is proud to present the third book in the Florenz Eisman Memorial Series—fine collections by New Jersey poets, notable or emerging. A gifted poet and great lover of poetry herself, Florenz was the publisher's partner in establishing the press and CavanKerry's Managing Editor from its inception in 2000 until her passing in 2013. Her ideas and intelligence were a great source of inspiration for writers and staff alike as were her quick wit and signature red lipstick.

CavanKerry Press is grateful for the support it receives from the New Jersey State Council on the Arts.

Also by Catherine Doty

Just Kidding (1999)
Momentum (2004)

For Renée Ashley

Contents

I

Breathing Underwater

Florida's just a thumb on a jigsaw puzzle,
but underwater the Weeki Watchee Mermaids
pour their tea, cook, exercise, iron clothes, guzzle
with muscular skill their Grapette soda,
with only occasional surreptitious sucks
on an air hose hidden in shell-studded scenery.
They grin, open eyes afloat in their blue-lit skulls.
Holding my breath was a skill I practiced, too,
like when I was ten years old and woke to a body
lowering onto my body, and a breath that put me in mind
of a rotten leg, a thing I'd seen in a book once
and which scared me, but not as much as this body
on top of my body, these digging fingers. I was wildly aware
that the room I was in was a pigsty, and I was a pig to be sleeping
in my clothes, and I wanted to blame it on someone, which
would have meant speaking, which I could not do—
it would have been too real—and I was too old to blame anyone
anyway. I closed my eyes to make the black world
blacker. The lamp was within my reach, and a railroad spike
I could easily have lifted, and also a bowling ball I'd found
on the tracks, but all I could think of was being ashamed
and dirty, and grateful the whole thing was happening
in black and white, like those mermaids on TV, their lips
and nails a black I knew was red, their long white legs
safely fused in their glistening tails.

For Thomas Mosby

I was kept with the lunches and snow boots
and dying plant in the corner of the classroom
farthest from others, the better to contain
my smell and filth, my calling out, my constant
bobbing and scribbling, but even I froze
when Sister Rose declared that although, believe
her, she tried to stop it, tomorrow a Negro, a boy,
would join our class. Up till then the one brown face
in the room was a photo: the heathen infant we bought
with a hundred nickels, whose soul we saved.

When the next day, just before prayers, Thomas Mosby
appeared, he studied his stiff black shoes and balled
his fists, while Sister Rose, with an energy new to her,
swung a desk next to mine and pointed him to it.
Our classmates groaned, not in anger but sympathy,
which I hoped Thomas Mosby knew was for him, not me,
and when our eyes somehow met I knew he was kin,
another ten-year-old who'd like to die, so I passed him
the apple I'd filched from some brown bag, and he took it,
though I had touched it, and ate it, too, and by recess we
were *nigger* and *nigger lover*, him with the face of a five-dollar
pagan baby, and me, who had cost him salvation,
with no face at all.

Sweet Ants

November 12th, and still the ants are here,
still skirt the butter searching for the sweet.
A swarm round a drop of syrup draws a crowd
like a lynching did in my namesake great-grandma's
time, when she fought to part the crowd to reach
the rope, and pluck it, which meant good luck
for her unborn child, but was elbowed aside
and trampled, and my great uncle, born there and then
in a pile of yellow leaves, soon was dead as the ants
I now thumb-smash or squirt with Windex, the ants
in their soldierly trail on the kitchen counter, dispersing
like a family and its stories, thinning and reaching
the cracks where they disappear, an elapsed-time shot
of the culprits, an aerial view, in which each apocryphal tale
equals every other, so one young great-grandpa, gut-shot
for stealing a mule, is no different from the one who
fiddled dances, or the aunt who first employed pink toilet paper,
or the nieces who could not resist its delicate beauty,
and wrapped it about themselves, and, thus festooned,
climbed onto their towel-draped chairs for Christmas dinner,
or the one with religious visions, a heart-shaped birthmark,
a Jewish nose, or a plate of steel in his head, like Cousin Jim,
who once, in France, forgot to wear his helmet, because
of which his heart was purple too, or my mother, who trips
on the dog as she heads to the table, a pineapple upside-down cake
in her hands, which she hugs as she rights herself, and how we
howl at the sight of her bulls-eye, pineapple-cherry-tipped tits,
as ants sweep in waves to the still-warm sugar-caked pan,
drawn like a hastening crowd to a flaming tree.

Tumbled

What in hell are you doing
at night on the creepiest street
in South Paterson fussing with some
battery-busted wreck of a pink Barbie jeep
you found in the weeds and think you can
get to run? Oh yeah, you live there, but still,
underneath a streetlamp, alone, the summer
each phrase you hear gets tossed in your head
till the sounds reverse, so *candy bar* morphs
into *bandy car*, and *starts at four* emerges *farts
at store*, and you, consumed, ignore the spank
of steps and don't look up, though you feel
the shadow's arcing fingers touch you,
and sooner than you can summon *Dun! Dun!
Ranger!* the real hands behind the darkness
pluck you up, and round your neck a thick arm
wraps itself. You hear *I have a knife, don't make
no noise*, but *knife* and *noise* both start
with the same sound, though *he kite mill me*
works, and this is a blade all right, its point
where your shirt and shorts are parting ways,
but he is new at this, fumbles to knead your front
with his knifeless hand, and you drop your dead weight
to the gravel then fake him out, and escape
with a few minor cuts and an earful of slobber,
and he doesn't get what you know he really wants,
so you run a victory lap through the crab apple trees,
past pricker bushes, beer cans, some bum's
wet mattress, screaming, shirtless, triumphant,
a *geyser whirl*.

Grandma

Mischief made her lift her arms and turn
with such a look of wonder on her face
that I was not afraid to see the flames
licking along both sleeves of her flannel robe,
but stepped back, as one does from an act
of God, the better to take in her glittering
pale green eyes, her pirate's nose, the few
yellow teeth in her little open mouth,
as my mother, her own mouth open
in a scream, rushed up behind her to yank
off the blazing robe and dance on its burning,
and Grandma, naked, jubilant, winked at me
while the kettle shrieked its way to boiling dry,
and sent me from some far hilltop in her far world
a vision of what it was certain I'd become:
wild-eyed and crazy and blazing like a six-gun,
nothing at all to be met with shame or fear.
So this is for her, who now has long been ash,
a chronicle the last word of which is *oh*.

The First Time I Was Told
to Fuck Myself

If he was playing possum,
he played well—cupped paws
curled in self-reference,
tongue limp in a head
shaped to divot the very air.
There, I'd been told, was a meal
for a smart black family,
with possum gravy, buttered grits
and biscuits, and something green
long stewed with salted pork.
And so I presented him (he was a him,
playing possum on his back
in the tallest weeds) to Roscoe,
our neighbor, kind Roscoe
who dragged home iron
and lengths of pipe,
and could be seen sinking
his dark hands into our trash cans.

Long after the ugly words,
the flying bottle,
long after this shame
grew blunted by other shames,
I carried with me that meal
I had envisioned, and the fear
as I lugged that creature
by his tail, not that he might
be dead, but that he might
not be, might thrust up

his punishing head and slash
my hands, then zig into the traffic
of Marshall Street, never to waken,
headless, skinless, gutless,
in a perfumed and oily pan
on a bed of sweet roots,
to be praised and divided,
to be divided and praised.

Wonderama

She may have been barely four,
but already she knew
that the people she watched on TV
could see her too, and the smiling
man she wanted for herself
she shared with a million kids
around the world. But she alone
saw past the corny songs,
the snapping suspenders,
to the lonely soul who needed
a little girl. Many days, as she
got dressed in the living room,
she'd look up quick from the sock
she was pulling on, and catch him
staring square into her face,
and once he swung a pointed
finger at her, a sharp jab that
made her hop behind a chair
then reappear, a little
at a time, to summon his eyes again,
to see if he missed her.

The Dawn of Beauty

He spins his scissors like a cowboy twirls a pistol
and chops off my braids, two snakes he rescues me from.
They lie on the kitchen floor among the crayons, near
a drawing I made of the famous Paterson Falls.

Downtown, at Saint Ag's Bingo, my mom yells *goddammit!*
as do all the women who do not win this round. I rub my head
where two circles of bare scalp tingle, and stare up at my father's
blurry mouth, which is saying *I hate all women with long hair.*

All princesses, all witches, Aunt Pauline—these are the kind that I
no longer am, the kind he cares enough to make me not. Then the shouting
starts, and I know my mother's home. He hollers *Who even looks*
at some little shit's hair? and *Make sure everybody knows she cut it herself.*

In the morning my mother gussies me up in a dress. Incongruous
as a chimp in my yellow ruffles, I follow her to the barber to fix
what's left. *Never*, he says, *let a four-year-old near the scissors,*
then laughs when I blame my dad, then shaves my head.

Behind Bars

Look, the lion likes you
was all I needed to hear,
that what drew him to the bars
was my good smell, me
in my string-shouldered playsuit,
little plaid sausage.

Today I read about my chiropractor,
how he stalked a forty-one-year-old
female patient, and threatened to lay
waste her marriage with texts
out of context.

How awful to squander attention—
the unresponsive so cool in their
craved flesh, so vastly ungrateful.

I remember Dr. Hearn leaning hard
on my shoulder, leaving me at dusk
on a manic couch, under the vinyl
of which waves of punishing thuddings
promised, if not relief, a different pain.

It was not my meat that the lion's
gold eyes grew great for,
but the horse chunk in the tub
being hoisted past me, sparkling
flies attendant in bright song.

II

What Does Not Kill Us

We were watching cartoons and each other,
alone together, my grandmother, gentle
and aphasic, losing her words at the rate
I was finding mine, who had just acquired
dementia and *diabetes*, two mouthfuls
of rhythmic sound with, as yet, no meaning.

A dog spoke harshly to another dog,
then a ton weight dropped out of the sky
and crushed him flat. He popped up
and skittered away, not one bit diminished.

My orders were to not let her turn on
the stove, to make her go to the bathroom,
and, *most important,* my mother whispered,
as she passed me the roll of candy with which
I was paid, *don't let Grandma have any:*
sugar will kill her. Then Mom kissed me
on the head and she was gone.

A cigar exploded and blackened a fat man's
face, then the smoke disappeared and his face
was white again. Grandma poked at the air
for words with the finger that scared me, the one
she sewed through at thirteen in the silk mill,
the one with a nail as thick and curved
as a cashew, and grunted *fire stick* like a TV Injun.

Then she laughed at a stuttering pig
in a porkpie hat, maybe because he had trouble
talking, too, and a gun shot out a flag with the word

BOOM on it. I placed a yellow candy on the table
between us. Grandma, her eyes never leaving
the flickering pictures, swiped it into her mouth
and crunched it gone with the punishing new
false teeth she kept in her pocket. Two greens
followed, an orange, and two more yellows.

Grandma sat there not dying while mice whapped
cats with bricks, and a cow in a polka dot dress
made eyes at a horse. The living continued:
dying was a lie, like *pick your nose and get
worms*, or *wear your snow boots inside
and get a headache*. Two mice danced a tango
on checkered linoleum, then wrestled a stolen pie
through a hole in a wall.

Grandma clenched the arms of her chair and lurched
to her feet, then did a cartoon dance on shaking legs,
then stared into my eyes and bit the air, then fell
to the strenuous business of finding words. She gasped,
at last, *pig pink*, and added, *now*.

When my mother came back, we were eating Spam on crackers,
wordlessly, in the way of immortal women. A wolf stepped
backwards off the edge of a cliff, and stood there a second,
not knowing enough to fall.

Half-Day Kindergarten

He sips from a can of flat beer and digs in the ashtray,
picking out butts still long enough to smoke,
and so doesn't have to borrow from the neighbors
to keep his mother in her freckled skin, and she,
in a waft of fumes, can relax and gossip,
which she does in encrypted language meant
to confound him, to arc over his five-year-old head
like so many lawn darts.

Mike thinks we don't know that he knows
where Her Highness was, Rosa Robideaux got that thing
lopped off, Chet Buckley boinked Vera P in the Rayburns' Cutlass.

He doesn't care what she wants him not to know:
that *Tess tried the turpentine trick on number five.*
Her voice in its rhythmic richness makes him tender.
He's thrilled to be her kid, her little goat. He delights
to swallow tin cans, like all goats do, and bends
at the waist, despite his tin-filled gut, to wait for his sister
the bitch to come home from high school, and wreck
all this joy with her screams that no one understands her.
He will rock just outside the door on his cloven hooves.
He will knock her down hard in the dirt with his savage horns.

The Mikado, 1960

My mother loves variation on a theme: jazzy pop tunes crooned
as spongy ballads by slack-jawed goofballs who suddenly can sing,
white peaches, black pansies, the litter's one long-haired kitten.
But when Groucho takes the stage, I watch her cringe: under the pancake
makeup it's still him, finger of shoeblack under the cheese-wedge nose,
crabbed shuffling in place of dancing, free hand stabbing the air
with no cigar. They've rigged him a big black hairdo (he plays Ko-Ko);
in silk he hunches, gobbling the scenery. My mother hoots in disgust,
but I don't mind: I'm eight, have a cup of coffee, will stay up till midnight.
Look at her, libretto in her lap, carping about too-long pauses for jokes
to sink in, the worn-out wall-eyed stare at Pitti-Sing, the dirty double takes
at Peep-Bo and Yum-Yum. This night I cherish. These I find heartening:
her disappointment, the heart of gold in her beer.

Catching

Despite health experts saying the vaccine is highly effective and safe, some parents are still choosing instead to expose children to chicken pox the old-fashioned way—with an infection party.

—*Katie Dangerfield,* Global News

A pariah when she is well, but in sickness desired,
a girl of eight douses herself with Evening in Paris,
dumps Cheez-Its out on a tin tray blissful with bluebirds,
and quivers with worth, and scratches, and tries to not scratch.
Blooming with blisters, she breaks out the Scrabble Junior.

The other children arrive at six o'clock to damply handle
the tiles and turn the cards. They sip from the one glass
of apple juice provided, tell her her looks are improved
by the clusters of sores, tally the minutes until their parents
return. Addled with fever, she registers only joy.

Within two weeks, two-thirds of third-graders are absent.
She counts the empty desks with nascent pride.
Mouths dry as hymnals, tongues too sore for speech,
they writhe in fever who soon will return to taunt her,
each familiar face souvenired with scars.

Gnomon

Softly lit in a murk of amniotic dust, the only two faces in the hallway of
  Saint Ag's School:
a clock with its echoing voice and shifty hands, and a girl, in a cloud of
  perplexity
and distinction: the only third-grader who cannot learn to tell time.
Told to return only when she can name the hour, she watches the red hand
hiccup around the track, and the longer black one skip forward, click by
  click,
and the shorter black one, like her, not do much at all. Teachers lean from
  their doorways
to witness her fecklessness, then turn, like the painted figures in cuckoo
  clocks, to vanish
into the movements of their classrooms. She's as likely to grasp the time
  as to knit a sock.

Standing and dozing, she jumps at the bell for prayers, those words she
  knows by rote
if not by heart, that are spoken each day at this time just as God likes to
  hear them,
with Thou and Thee, and sorry we sinned again. She's been praying
  already for hours
for understanding, which, like the pony she begged for all last year, she
  realizes

she never will possess, but still, since it's time to address the all-knowing
    Father,
whose workings, like the clock's, are a mystery, the girl casts her small
    shadow
and weeps for a miracle, and covers her glowing face with obedient hands.

Standing, 1964

See her clothes as they drop in the yellow weeds—
tee shirt and shorts in the upraised arms of the yarrow.
Her arms are lifted, too—she exults or prays—
she is narrow and flat, her skin white as surrender.
The thatchy back of her head is a patch of knots,
her teeth are rotted, but, then, so are theirs, bared
as the boys reach to touch her, not unkindly.
They are sixteen, and she is half their age. Above them
a star goes dark, or many darken—a sky-cleaving jet
unfurls four slender trails. She feels like the pinecone seed
that split the boulder, the bullet exploding the head
of the president: once invisible, once inconsequential,
now singular, at last in her rightful place.

Touch

She stayed to see the werewolf movie end, then was too scared to cross
the cool dark grass, the scuffed bare dirt where Duke was chained all day,
to get back home, and so she stayed and stayed until they had no choice
but throw her out.

Across the yards the other kids were sent to form a human chain and bring
her back, hand by familiar hand, a rustic dance, until the growling creature
she feared would tear her, the man the moon reduced to fangs and fur,
returned to his lair a sad and thwarted beast, and all the neighbors slept
in gentle peace, except for Jack Finch, who knew which window was hers.

Easy-Bake

A pie the size of an eye patch, cakes
like checkers: the Easy-Bake oven
starts you out so small what you make
is a sniff and barely that.
What drives it is a light bulb, a mere idea,
but you want to *bake,* want to fist and wrestle
dough and slather icing, want to wobble
the first fat slice to a flowered plate.

Sprawled in the wading pool, the drunk upstairs
sours the summer air with his grunts and snores,
his jutting feet for only the rugged to see.

You want to back, bent at the waist,
from a two-toned car, with a glistening cake
pink-frosted in peaky licks. When you turn
and they see it, the world will *oooh*
like at fireworks.

Larval

They rest in silken nests in the crotches of trees,
until someone like you shows up with a big glass jar
and harvests them, warm handfuls of gentle pets,
and screws on the lid, which is punched full of jagged
holes, and takes them home and into bed with you.

Inside, each harbors a squirt of streaky goo, the colors
of every condiment at a cookout. Squirrels, bats, foxes,
and skunks are their natural enemies, as are children armed
with big glass jars.

When you are asleep, to reciprocate your love, they squeeze
through the punctured portals in the lid, leaving luscious tufts
of their soft brown coats, and crawl to your lips,
where they spend the night kissing you.

On your face in the morning: undulant eyebrows, tiny droppings
like scattered punctuation. Like you, not one will find itself
with wings, though one potential moth, too weak to travel,
remains in the jar, on a twist of wilted grass,
and stares up at the stars you made for her.

Migraine

Always the hiding, the searching for cool and darkness.
Sometimes wrapped up in the shed in a roll of oilcloth
to conjure, by way of distraction, good names for black ponies,
sometimes face-first in the frost of a cobbled igloo, sometimes
actual sleep or a throbbing stupor, or hours spent sucking the rot
from a bad back tooth.

And in spring, when heralds of light sling wavering halos,
when dandelions and storm-colored violets thrum, when even
the scent of mint makes the stomach roil, to dig like my dog
in the damp dirt under the pear tree, and there to lie still,
with a popsicle on my head.

Dirt Cellar

Skull-and-crossboned
bottles in a spice rack.

Wads of novena booklets
tied with twine.

Some kind of engine,
rusted cans of paint,
caustic jelly to pry open
with a file.

Also a few dank nests
of rag and straw,

and the scratch and squeak
of the rat we call Father Rodent,
piebald black and white
with a Roman collar.

Riding the Maniac

Our mother hollers, *Look at that maniac!*
It's low, blackish-green, three-cars-long
and as wide as this street, a carnival ride
on wheels. (I assume, of course, that *maniac*
is its name, though my mother's howl referred
to the sharp left-hand turn.)

You find these things in desperate, no-carnival times,
parked on the gravely grass at backyard parties.
Inside, three painted bowls lurch around a track,
each barely holding three kids and the noise they make.

But no matter how fast you spin, there's just no breeze.
By any other name, it's hotter than church, though only
half as likely to make you throw up. The driver, my mother
tells us, is a *pervert*, which we guess means a guy
who drives maniacs for a living.

III

Flag

You step in shit, you sit on broken glass—

it's just another playday on the street.

You tissue-wad the place that stings and bleeds

and stuff the bloody pants in some clogged drawer

your mother chances on that afternoon,

which is why now what looks like a Japanese flag

dangles from her left hand as her right one grabs you.

Odd as it is to have her to yourself (the little sisters

off in a neighbor's yard), stranger still is her look

of queasy stupefaction, the cigarette locked and twitching

between her lips, as she croaks in a gust of smoke

and profundity, *You are a woman now*,

and you say, *Oh shit*, though you are only nine,

and nothing is said at all about the shorts, or what

a woman does that you must learn, or how to proceed

now that childhood is behind you, on this day

that somehow you find yourself grown up,

a fact as surprising as sitting on broken glass.

Switch

Not counting three laps round a cordoned ring of dust
on a Shetland pony with one white eye, like a seer,
this is her first experience on horseback.
She hopes she gets the spotted one. She does.
In her pocket: a rolled-up willow switch.

She seeks the adhesive gravity of cowboys,
what keeps them glued to their saddles in the Westerns,
and also, apparently, helps them keep their hats.
A galloping horse rides as smooth as a flying carpet.

Of course, at the first faint touch of the willow whip,
the Appaloosa swings up like a Murphy bed,
bolts into flight and flings her to the ground, where she grazes
on the straw- and shit-filled mud, no kind of cowboy,
though, briefly, with her hat on, ten feet tall.

Gorillas

He held the head in his hands
and wept into it.
No window gave back his image;
he'd smashed them all—
through splits in the thick black leather
padding his fists, the white stuffing
poked like smoke.

Don was drunk,
of course, on Halloween,
and had spent all the grocery money
that was left after Sissy bought
and ate and bought again
the Payday bars she meant to give the kids,
on renting this stupid costume.

The head rocked on his knee and caught
his tears. What hurt him so?
That the neighbors he hoped to alarm
with his simian self, hidden, this time,
in a pelt of synthetic fuzz, weren't home
when he needed to hear their screams of fear?

Didn't he know that he scared us
best of all when he hollered and slammed
up the stairs at four a.m. and woke up
his boy and girls, who wailed to break glass
that they didn't want to sing, didn't want
to bang on pots till the dogs all howled,

wanted only to sleep through the years
till they could leave, wanted only to be like
the lucky kids downstairs, their father
distant and scornful: a better drunk.

At the Circus

As a red star grows in the sawdust
under his head, two clowns in flapping shoes

swoop in with a stretcher, and bear off
the spangled figure who fell from the sky.

In the ring to the left ladies dance on galloping horses;
to the right Chinese acrobats—twelve—on but one bike

cycle. In seconds the air refills with sparkling bodies
and, but for one flying man, all is whole again.

Salesman

I sweep dog hair off my pants with a Stanhome Valet,
a brush-and-shoehorn combo that sells itself
except where dogs and cats outnumber pants, like this
dead-end street at the foot of Garret Mountain, where
sales recruits are sent to pitch brushes and saucepans
and life insurance and Bibles and family portraits
to an inbred clan so sullen, so slack-jawed and squinty,
that census takers resort to ballpark figures. Left behind
on one gritty surface or another, a business card
rubber-stamped with the name *Joe Good*, which is not my name
but company code for *poor*. Though none will call, I can
claim each one as a contact. The dirt on my shoes from
their houses I wipe on the grass.

Federal Sweets & Biscuit, 1962

When they find him in the boiler room, facedown,
they think *dead*, or *drunk*, or *dead-drunk*, but there
is no bottle. They drag him out to the loading dock,
smack him alive, and drive him down to Saint Joe's,
where he laps, with a starving passion, a special air,
and nurses dive into the five-pound deluxe assortment,
deluxe meaning half of the cookies have chocolate or nuts.

The call comes that Dad has been poisoned at the plant.
We picture a butter cookie from Federal Sweets
topped with a skull and crossbones of hard white icing.
Maybe somebody slipped a powder into his coffee,
like that farting potion sold in the back of *Batman*.
No, we learn, carbon monoxide is finer than that,
more invisible than the airborne mist of sugar that
by day's end covers Dad's slicked-back hair in a drift.

At last, after dark, bashed fedora aslant on his head,
our father staggers in and looks round for his supper.
We've been told not to stare at him, bother him, make him
feel worse. His shoes appear the same with their spatters
of chocolate. His face looks like there's no worse way
he could feel. Where is the wall-slapping monster
who can't find his bed? Someone, get this good man
a big glass of milk.

Shaman

My father comes home in a bad
way and takes out the porch.
The house shakes. We wake up,
and all of the neighbors wake, too.
They gather outside in sleepy
twos and threes. A few hold a pet
or baby or a drink. One starts
to shout; the others shut her up.
Under the streetlight they watch
him shed his clothes: the shirt
he hangs on a railroad spike
stuck in a tree, the pants he folds
along where a crease would be
then rolls up and drops
in the gravel and chicory.
He stumbles over the shoes
he kicked off first. The motor
still runs, and the smashed lights
still hold their small flames.
Howls all around as the baggy
gray shorts are let go, then the hat,
smashed flat because cats like
to sleep on hats, is hung on
the mailbox. He slaps at himself
where he thinks his pockets
are, but no keys. Some asshole
starts to clap.

IV

Dusk

Evening proffers a pink lick
above Garret Mountain.

Translucent as a potholder:
Paterson's sky.

New Girl in Town

Cross the street, Franny, if ever you spy
Joe Moe, whose hand-hewn tar paper
shack we approach on bets, or pitch chunks
of pudding stone at from moving cars.
You'll want, too, to skirt Donna's uncles,
Drunk and Jolly, who'll sneak through
your screen door with snow cones and try
to kiss you, and Ronnie Vee, who just got out
of Rahway (we're not supposed to know
what got him there).

And Saint Ag's School is an iron maiden
of dangers, though statues of saints peer out
of each dusky corner, and Jesus his plaster self
tops the entrance stairs, where one day he stared
at a second-grader's vomit, hand held before
his exposed and flaming heart, as if to express
distaste for incarnation. Expect more shame
to be handed out than blessings, administered lavishly
both in word and deed: for girls, eighteen inches
of steel on open palms; for boys, once slung across
a nun's black lap, lusty whacks on the seats
of their regulation pants.

So, that's about it, Fran, except for that candy store
where the old guy gives out wax lips for Halloween
and ends of cold cuts to the dogs he lets inside.
He'll say, *Sweetheart, you look pale—are you on the rag?*
If you're hungry, Franny, tell him *yes.* He'll put his hand
on your stomach, and then on your forehead, then tell
you you're clammy, then toast you a piece of toast.

Franny Takes Advice

When somebody old enough
to be somewhat wise
tells Franny the way to survive
at Kennedy High
is to land the first blow
the second Evil approaches,
she does, having given no thought
to Evil's friends,
who sinister their way
into the bathroom, where soon,
in a litter of chewed gum
and cigarette butts, Gullibility lies
like Gulliver on the beach,
long black hair divided
to fill ten fists.

Franny of the Jungle

When the Grand Street Library
stupidly loans her books,
great numbers of which she pulls
in a Radio Flyer, she attracts, at once,
a mob of wagonless felons,
who kick the crap out of her shins
and take it all, including the book
she's renewed for seven months
about a lost girl who's learned
to live in the jungle, whose pillow
is a sleeping tiger's haunch,
who eats, without flinching, termites
twisting in honey, who hurtles, screaming,
through the world on a matrix of vines,
who never plods three miles home,
bookless, hair webbed with spit.

Condemned

I

Franny and I leave school with Debbie Nank, who's heard about
Franny's house and wants to see it, and maybe step inside
if she has the nerve, but because it's Friday, and Friday means
Kraft Macaroni, Franny runs the steep last block alone.

Debbie freezes when we reach Franny's slumping porch, the house
with its caving roof and glassless windows. She confides in me
that if that's where she had to live, she'd race to the footbridge
and hurl herself into the Falls. Then she asks me where I live,
which is downstairs from Franny.

II

Before waddling off to snooze in the dark all day, our mother's possum
peeks out from his hole in the wall, one seeded each evening with berries
and cold spaghetti, and night crawlers pried from the ground with a
     carving fork.

In volume O of a neighbor's *Funk & Wagnalls*, in dawn's primal light,
with coffee and some despair, she learns that the only marsupial in our
     country
(not to mention the first one ever to live in her kitchen) belongs to the
     least evolved
of all the species. Like her, for millions of years he hasn't changed.

But for now she takes solace in her possum's opposable thumbs,
the phalanx of fangs he bares in a pink-tongued yawn.
Soon her children will waken and plague her with their needs.

III

While Peggy draws John Lennon on the wall, I print, in magic marker
on the ceiling, a poem I love about poppies and the dead. Mary cracks
    black walnuts
with a rock, and feeds the pieces to our sister Judy, who pries the rusted lid
from a can of house paint so she and Tommy can camouflage their beds.

In the kitchen, our happy mother plays Nelson Eddy so loud that it
    drowns out
the screams of the couple upstairs. She is the reason, she tells us, why we
    are so smart,
and smarts you can't buy, or we'd sell ours and get a TV.

Hitter

We pick the gravel out of the fallen pears
and eat them with Wonder Bread and squirts of ketchup,
which, Franny, you learn to do because of me,
just like you learn to embroider and draw a horse.

And what do I learn from you? To avoid your father,
to not expect a hot dog when he cooks out. And, no offense,
but I can't eat your Mom's macaroni: it's served
in the dishpan she uses to shave her legs.

And when one day I share with you just what I think
of your brother (who you yourself say is as smart
as a carnival goldfish), you tell me my mother is old
and my nose is big, then punch me in my big nose

and turn and run, so I grab my baseball bat
and chase you home, kick open your front door
the second you slam it, and there sits your father
composing a mayonnaise sandwich, and not too happy

to find me dropping in. He hollers, *Hey! Where you going
with that damn bat?* And real fast I answer, *Oh, Franny
asked for it*, which, if you're honest, you have to admit is funny,
then I whack you in your pink curlers and run like hell.

V

Seaside Heights, 1964

Don't feel sorry for her, twelve-year-old
with one dime for the Boardwalk.
Just watch as she wins on the number fifteen,
color black, a guitar, also black, its lacquer
hot from the sun that baked it as it hung,
waiting to be won.

Watch some more as she joins the throngs
of sunburned winners, who hoist their life-sized
stuffed bears, their toaster ovens, their cartons
of Luckies and Camels and melted Clark Bars,
their Beatles albums and taffy and six-speed blenders.

The guitar has a slender neck strung with silver strings,
which she tips up in her left hand so as not to strike others.
The hole in its belly gives off a luscious scent.
It is shaped like a woman, which is more than she can say,
and she wears it as if she could play it, which she can't.

Fun

The second the clown-painted door slapped
closed behind me, I knew I'd screwed up again:
the moving floor could kill, and the turning barrel,
through which, in a certain cadence, one could pass,
was, for me, another deadly choice. I watched,
in the infinite twinkle of fly-specked lights, the damned
grope and slam through a room of confounding glass.

I clawed at the blind and handleless side of the door,
eventually made some purchase, and emerged,
ashamed, an unfortunate birth again, and as such was received
by a drunk and languorous boy, who did not look up,
who would not give back my quarter. I beheld then
in the heartless and undulant mirror a self I suspected
all saw and turned swiftly from: the twisted stump of a body,
the squatty legs, the terrible head full of gas or impossible kapok,
the bleary mouth sucking splinters from stinging fingers.

Here, Boy

Back when a kiss made me stagger,
I needed a dog. Not some ukulele-sized
poodle stuffed in a dress,

but a solid, bowlegged, he-man of a mutt,
a sidekick to love who would center and slow
and calm me, a dignified dog who'd set a good example,

one nothing at all like the hungry girl
who owns him, who languishes on the porch
with her tongue hanging out.

Sixteen, in the One Room That Locks

He sits on the open toilet. She faces him, straddles
the arctic rim of the claw-foot tub: they kiss and kiss
and drop their clothes and kiss. Around them in the dark,
shin-deep in the shallows, months of her family's fetid,
cast-off clothing. Crustaceans couldn't couple in this stench.
Then a loud drunken yell and a fist at the door—her dad.

The boy burrows face-first in that haystack of sulfurous rags.
The girl dips a hand to the floor, grabs a random garment;
more or less draped she kicks open the door and flees,
leaving the boy to the chilly grit of the floor, the tugging
belches and grunts, the stuttered stream. Tomorrow, she knows,
the boy will set free the story, every detail too bleak for hyperbole.

That's when the Earth, in response to her frenzied begging,
opens: the floor before her buckles and fractures,
and the cellar below, its dirt bed bifurcated, gives way
to the world's very center, which, black as Halloween lipstick,
lures her with its promise of relief. She allows herself one moment
of indecision, then closes her eyes and leaps from the beckoning lip
to drown in the lightless passion of Earth's kind heart
her shame and sorrow and loss and makeshift toga.

On Valley Road

The miles we trudge this morning, all uphill,
take us to Clifton, where kids have moms that work,
and the girls we want to be allow us in, provided
we're gone before their folks get home. But it's Sunday:
their families are just getting back from Mass, and we are
forbidden to enter those cool, screened-in porches.

We let our minds wander the shelves of a basement fridge,
one stocked with stacked-up bottles of beer and birch beer,
and one fifth of vodka twice watered to fruitlessness,
near a powder room papered in pink and yellow plaid,
where we took turns reading three pages of Mary McCarthy,
who knew a great deal about men and how to touch them.

We are hungry and bored and look forward to only more
boredom. When a station wagon bumps to a stop at the curb,
the driver waves at Coreen like he just must know her,
so she sticks her head in the car through the half-open window
then jerks it back out just the second he hits the gas, just before
her noggin pops off like a wooly grape, and her headless body,
long neck to horn-soled feet, collapses in a shroud of fishy exhaust,
and she lives to tell what she saw in that swirling moment:
the bird's nest of pale pink eggs in his unzipped lap,
though described in the book as a sort of thrumming snake,
was the selfsame, shape-shifting marvel we read about. Nothing
is open and all we have is two quarters, which a gumball machine
clogged with Beer Nuts screws us out of.

Working Girls

For Althea, Gladys, and Four-Way Annie

Like them, she excels at her game and is fairly fearless.
Like them, she endures the tedious for cash.
So, at seven p.m. when most sitters head to the suburbs,
she appears, with a sleeve of Fig Newtons and *Charlotte's Web*,
at the sprung and screenless door of town's busiest hookers,
who glance at her once, then pounce into their night.

How to describe the extent of the house's squalor—
sink tectonic and dicey with towering dishes, corners piled
with bottles, clothes, and shoes, and a smell, egg-rotten, easily traced
to its source: a girl, the victim of a recent Tonette home perm,
whose blistered scalp is martial with rows of curlers,
and babies, two, one clobbering the other, who rocks
on his hands and knees in a pizza box.
But for a few more flies, she could be home.

When the women return at two, she expects them to jingle,
at least the one she's heard does things for quarters,
but Annie's the one who pays her in rolled-up dollars, who waves
at her from the window like someone's mom. There's nothing, really,
worth telling those other sitters, who worked tonight
for good people in fancy houses, then scattered before the dads
tried to drive them home.

JC and Me in the Summer of '64

Catholicism and puberty duked it out the summer my body
broke out of its corral and galloped Paterson's streets
in search of sugar through the new and luscious grasses
of impure thought.

The priest I confessed to dismissed me as *overly scrupulous*—
I was thinking too much about thinking of dirty things—
and, distracted because the word *scrupulous* started with *screw*,
I left with a head full of sin and two Holy Cards, which he passed
me as if they were discards in Holy Strip Poker, a game I imagined
instructive and entertaining.

The first was Saint Agatha, Sicily's virgin martyr, her eyes
rolled up to God, as often mine were. She would not renounce
Him despite the terrible tortures He could, being God, have simply
plucked her from. If it were me, I'd have just said *Jesus who?*
then cantered right out of there with my virgin self, and ducked
behind the bleachers at Hinchliffe Stadium.

The second Holy Card was Jesus Himself, bathed in a golden light
and softly smiling, halo tipped back and eyes beaming mercy
and mirth. I hadn't noticed till then how handsome He was:
eyes like blue poppies, a nose I regarded with envy, wavy auburn hair
with a center part. I pictured the halls of Saint Ag's full of boys in kaftans,
and me, with my black hair tossing, in the hot pink short shorts
that got me suspended from school.

Imagine, I thought, when He, too, was confused and changing, not quite
a man yet, and almost, but not quite, God. Hear me calling His name,
though He's already heading toward me, the August wind blowing

His robe between His legs, the power to miracle lighting His holy face,
a gingery fuzz on His lip, and an eager smile telling me I have powers, too.

At my nearness His thoughts will cleave the Paterson Falls, send beer cans
    and tires
jouncing down McBride, and cause the all-the-way hot dogs at Libby's Lunch
to vault like angels from their very secret sauce.

Acknowledgments

I would like to thank the editors of the publications in which these poems first appeared, sometimes in different versions:

The Literary Review: "Behind Bars," "Breathing Underwater," "The First Time I Was Told to Fuck Myself," "Gorillas," "Standing, 1964," "Sweet Ants"
Referential Magazine: "Easy-Bake," "Here, Boy"
Shrew: "Dusk"
Tiferet: "Grandma"
Welcome to the Resistance: Poetry as Protest: "The Dawn of Beauty," "For Thomas Mosby"

Heartfelt gratitude to all at CavanKerry Press, especially to Joan Cusack Handler, whose faith, vision, and friendship made this volume possible, and to Gabriel Cleveland for his wise and thoughtful guidance. Great appreciation to Dimitri Reyes for his thoughtfulness, to Ryan Scheife for his gorgeous cover design, and to the indefatigable Joy Arbor, who held every word up to the light and checked every fact.

Special thanks to Martin Farawell, Ysabel Gonzalez, and past and present members of the Geraldine R. Dodge Foundation.

Loving gratitude to Renée Ashley, Wendy Barnes-Thomassen, Aliki Barnstone, Robert Carnevale, Maribeth Cassels, Dolores Choteborsky, Peggy Choteborsky, Flower Conroy, Judith Cooper, Joan Crowe, Diana Goetsch, Linda Hillringhouse, Mark Hillringhouse, Mel Kershaw, Erica Mosner, Peter Murphy, Mary Doty Neadle, Priscilla Orr, Lisa Rhoades, Susanna Rich,

Ken Ronkowitz, Denise Rue, Mimi Schwartz, Adrienne and Jim Thomas, Herb Way, and Pat Whitehouse.

Endless gratitude, with much love, to my sisters and brothers Ray, Brad, Patricia, Peggy, Mary, Judy, and Tom, to their families, and to Ali, Tom, and the incandescent Natalie.

Love and love to Henry, Will, and my husband Fred.

Sincere gratitude to the National Endowment for the Arts and the New Jersey State Council on the Arts for their encouragement and support.

Lastly, a sincere and fervent thank you to my students and teachers, and to all the friends who ever helped me move. You know who you are.

CavanKerry's Mission

A not-for-profit literary press serving art and community, CavanKerry is committed to expanding the reach of poetry and other fine literature to a general readership by publishing works that explore the emotional and psychological landscapes of everyday life, and to bringing that art to the underserved where they live, work, and receive services.

Other Books in the Florenz Eisman Memorial Series

Wonderama has been set in Skolar Latin, a robust text typeface designed to address the needs of serious typography. Its letterforms follow conventional proportions allowing for comfortable reading and maintains credibility while incorporating a subtle personal style. It was designed by David Březina and published by Rosetta Type Foundry.